My State
MASSACHUSETTS

By Christina Earley

TABLE OF CONTENTS

A Crabtree Seedlings Book

Crabtree Publishing
crabtreebooks.com

School-to-Home Support for Caregivers and Teachers

This book helps children grow by letting them practice reading. Here are a few guiding questions to help the reader build his or her comprehension skills. Possible answers appear in red.

Before Reading:

- What do I know about Massachusetts?
    - *I know that Massachusetts is a state.*
    - *I know that Massachusetts is a historic place.*
- What do I want to learn about Massachusetts?
    - *I want to learn which famous people were born in Massachusetts.*
    - *I want to learn what the state flag looks like.*

During Reading:

- What have I learned so far?
    - *I have learned that Boston is the state capital of Massachusetts.*
    - *I have learned that President John F. Kennedy was born in Massachusetts.*
- I wonder why...
    - *I wonder why the state flower is the mayflower.*
    - *I wonder why the baseball park is called Fenway Park.*

After Reading:

- What did I learn about Massachusetts?
    - *I have learned that the Berkshires have many waterfalls.*
    - *I have learned that the state dog is the Boston terrier.*
- Read the book again and look for the glossary words.
    - *I see the word **capital** on page 6, and the word **production** on page 11. The other glossary words are found on pages 22 and 23.*

MASSACHUSETTS
Hi! My name is Logan. Welcome to Massachusetts!

I live in Boston. There are many old, historic buildings next to new ones.

My city **invented** Dunkin' Donuts!

Massachusetts is in the northeastern United States. The **capital** is Boston.

Fun Fact: Boston is the largest city in Massachusetts.

The state dog is the Boston terrier.

The mayflower is
the state flower.

We catch a lot of **seafood** in Massachusetts. Clam chowder is delicious.

Fun Fact: Massachusetts is one of the top states for seafood **production** in the U.S.

My state flag is white. The state **seal** is in the middle.

There are five national sports teams in Massachusetts.

I can go back in time at Old Sturbridge Village. I pretend I live in the 1830s.

Fun Fact: Old Sturbridge Village is the largest outdoor history museum in the Northeast.

HARTFORD & WORCESTER

I pick apples in Johnny Appleseed Country.

I have fun watching a baseball game at Fenway Park.

Author Dr. Seuss was born in Massachusetts. **Founding Father** Benjamin Franklin was also born in Massachusetts.

Fun Fact: President John F. Kennedy was born in Brookline, Massachusetts.

My favorite beaches are in Cape Cod.

I look for waterfalls when I go hiking in the Berkshires.

Glossary

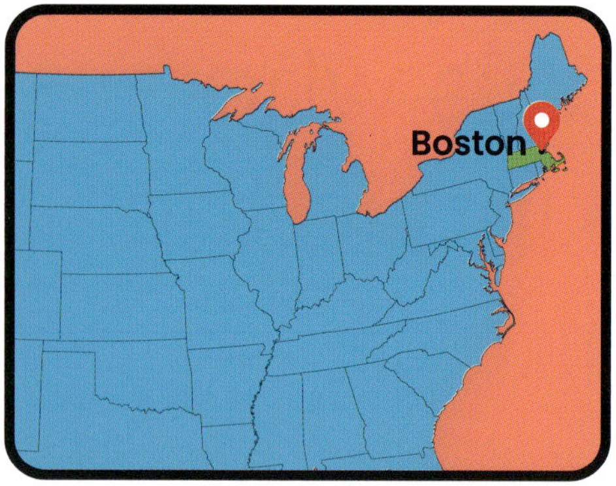

capital (cap-ih-tuhl): The city or town where the government of a country, state, or province is located

Founding Father (fown-ding fah-ther): One of the American colonists who worked together to lead the American Revolution and build a new government

invented (in-ven-tid): Created

production (pro-duk-shin): Preparing and making something to sell

seafood (see-food): Fish and shellfish from the ocean that is used for food

seal (seel): A special design that is used on important papers and other items

Index

About the Author

Christina Earley lives in sunny South Florida with her husband and son. She enjoys traveling around the United States and learning about different historical places. Her hobbies include hiking, yoga, and baking.

Written by: Christina Earley
Designed and Illustrated by: Bobbie Houser
Series Development: James Earley
Proofreader: Melissa Boyce
Educational Consultant: Marie Lemke M.Ed.

Photographs:
Alamy: Schoening: p. 14; John Woodworth: p. 14-15; Archive PL: p. 18 left; Pictorial Press Ltd: p. 19
Newscom: Marty Jean-Louis/Sipa USA: p. 13
Shutterstock: Sean Pavone: cover, 4; Allan Wood Photography: p. 3; Nickolastock: p. 5, 22; Volina: p. 6, 22; GagliardiPhotography: p. 7; Eve Photography: p. 8; Tom Meaker: p. 9; Maya K. Photography: p. 10-11, 23; norikko: p. 11, 23; Box Lab: p. 12, 23; Jorge Salcedo: p. 16; Eric Broder Van Dyke: p. 17; Stocksnapper: p. 18 right, 22; Cindy Goff: p. 20; Colin D. Young: p. 21

Crabtree Publishing

crabtreebooks.com 800-387-7650

Printed in the U.S.A./012023/CG20220815

Published in Canada
Crabtree Publishing
616 Welland Avenue
St. Catharines, Ontario
L2M 5V6

Published in the United States
Crabtree Publishing
347 Fifth Avenue
Suite 1402-145
New York, New York, 10016

Library and Archives Canada Cataloguing in Publication
Available at Library and Archives Canada

Library of Congress Cataloging-in-Publication Data
Available at the Library of Congress

Hardcover: 978-1-0396-9659-4
Paperback: 978-1-0396-9766-9
Ebook (pdf): 978-1-0396-9980-9
Epub: 978-1-0396-9873-4